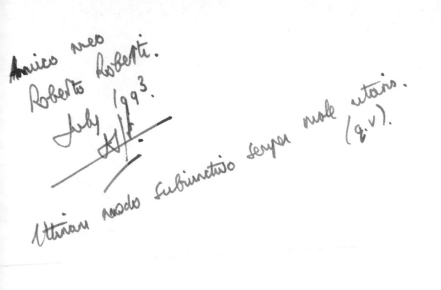

Amico meo
Roberto Roberti.
July 1993.

Uttinam nosdo subiunctivo serpen male utaris. (q.v.).

LATIN FOR ALL OCCASIONS

Lingua Latina Occasionibus Omnibus

LINGUA LATINA OCCASIONIBUS OMNIBUS

HENRICUS BARBATUS SCRIPSIT

ANGUS
& ROBERTSON

An Imprint of HarperCollins*Publishers*

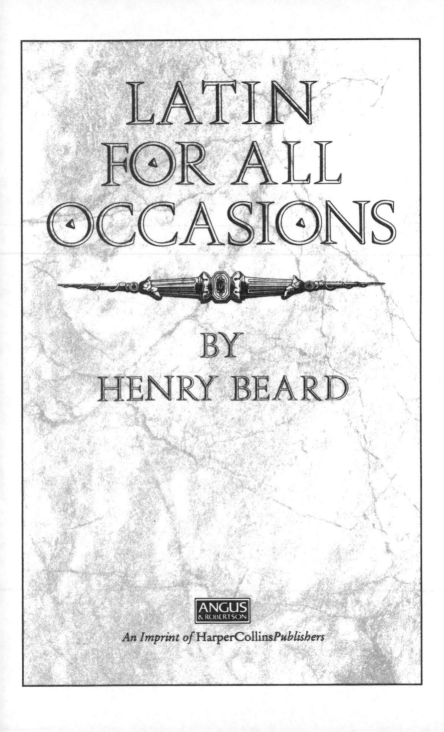

LATIN FOR ALL OCCASIONS

BY
HENRY BEARD

ANGUS
& ROBERTSON

An Imprint of HarperCollins*Publishers*

AN ANGUS & ROBERTSON BOOK

First published in the United Kingdom by
Angus & Robertson (UK) in 1991
An imprint of HarperCollinsPublishers Ltd
Reprinted 1992, 1993
First published in the United States by Villard Books, a division
of Random House, Inc., New York, in 1990

Angus & Robertson (UK)
77-85 Fulham Palace Road, London W6 8JB United Kingdom
Collins/Angus & Robertson Publishers Australia
Unit 4, Eden Park, 31 Waterloo Road,
North Ryde, NSW 2113, Australia
William Collins Publishers Ltd
31 View Road, Glenfield, Auckland 10, New Zealand

British Library Cataloguing in Publication Data—available
from the publisher

ISBN 0 207 17125 4

Printed and bound in Great Britain by
HarperCollinsManufacturing Glasgow

Was I speaking Latin again?
Denuone Latine loquebar?

Silly me. Sometimes it just sort of slips out.
Me ineptum. Interdum modo elabitur.

PREFACE
Praefatio

You know the feeling all too well. There you are, chatting with business associates at an upscale watering hole, or participating in a little good-natured give-and-take during a golf or tennis match, or relaxing with friends on the beach, or maybe just reviewing the day with your family at the supper table. You spot a chance to liven up the discussion with a particularly pithy observation in Latin, and then, all of a sudden, you're assailed by paralyzing doubts.

Is the verb you were going to use in the second or third conjugation? Is it irregular? Deponent? Reflexive? Defective? Does it take *ut* and a subjunctive or an infinitive with an accusative? Or, worse still, does it take the dative? Would a gerundive construction be more appropriate, or laughably awkward? How about a passive periphrastic or—but no, it's too late. The moment has passed, the conversation has moved on.

Now be honest—how many times has that happened to you? If you answer is *saepius* (too often)—and we bet it is!—then *Lingua Latin Occasionibus Omnibus* (Latin for All Occasions) is the book for you.

Here, in one handy, easy-to-use volume, are hundreds of everyday English expressions rendered into grammatically accurate, idiomatically correct classical Latin, just as you would have translated them yourself if you had the time. And all of these practical phrases are conveniently organized into familiar conversational categories so that you can be confident that in any social situation some suitable Latin *bona dicta* (bon mots) will be right at your fingertips, just the way they would be if you could only get in a little practice.

The next time you feel like using the immortal language of Caesar, Cicero, Virgil, and Horace to turn an ordinary remark into a timeless utterance, don't let *feles, felis, feli, felem, fele* (the cat) get your tongue. With a copy of *Lingua Latina Occasionibus Omnibus* (Latin for All Occasions) in your toga, you'll never again be intimidated by those seven hundred verb endings, ninety noun cases, and twenty kinds of ablative. And you'll quickly discover that whether you want to impress the boss, entertain your friends, keep the kids in line, or charm that special someone, speaking Latin is as easy as taking Gaul from the Gauls!

    Bona fortuna! (Good luck!)

ACKNOWLEDGMENTS
Gratiae

I would like to thank Mark Sugars and Winifred Lewellen, who reviewed my Latin for accuracy and appropriateness. Their many corrections and suggestions greatly improved this book, and no doubt spared me untold grief from outraged Latin teachers. To these two distinguished classical scholars belongs much of the credit for any felicity of style or elegance of diction; the *culpa* for any mistakes is entirely *mea*.

CONTENTS

Quad in libro continetur

INTRODUCTION:
A BRIEF GUIDE TO
LATIN PRONUNCIATION

*Prooemium: Locutio linguae Latinae
paucis verbis explanatur*

If it's been a few years since you last conversed in Latin regularly,
your pronunciation may have gotten a bit rusty, so we've included
here a short summary of the basics of the spoken language just to
help you brush up a little.

A word of caution: This is a simplified system of pronunciation
for colloquial Latin based in part on modern Italian, the direct
vernacular descendant of the everyday speech of ancient Rome. If
you're planning to give a formal oration or a reading from one of
the great works of classical literature, you're obviously going to
want to consult the standard scholarly reference books for the
proper literary pronunciation.

I VOWELS AND A FEW DIPTHONGS

Sure, I speak a little Latin.
- *Sane, paululum linguae Latinae dico.*
  SAH-nay, pow-LOO-luhm LEEN-gwye Lah-TEE-nye DEE-koh.

  A is pronounced "ah" as in "f<u>a</u>ther."
  E is pronounced "ay" as in "th<u>ey</u>," but the very common words
     <u>et</u> (and), <u>est</u> (is), and <u>sed</u> (but) should be pronounced like "b<u>et</u>,"
     "b<u>est</u>," and "s<u>aid</u>," and the very common word ending <u>em</u>
     should be pronounced like "st<u>em</u>."

I is pronounced "ee" as in "Vaseline," but the very common words id (it) and in (in, on) should be pronounced like "did" and "din."

O is pronounced "oh" as in "go."

U is pronounced "oo" as in "crude," but the very common word endings us and um shuld be pronounced like "puss" and "room" (with the "oo" sound of "cookbook"), and the very common word ut (how, so that) should be pronounced like "put."

AE is a dipthong (a pair of vowels joined together to form a single sound) pronounced "eye."

AU is a dipthong pronounced "ow," as in "luau."

OE is a dipthong pronounced "oy."

II CONSONANTS

I picked it up here and there. Really, Latin isn't all that hard.

• *Id legi modo hic modo illic. Vero, Latine loqui non est difficilissimum.*

IDD LAY-gee MOH-doh HEEK MOH-doh EEL-leek. WAY-roh, Lah-TEE-nay LOH-kwee NOHN EHSST dee-fee-kee-LEESE-see-muhm.

B, D, F, H, K, L, M, N, P, and Z all sound the same as they do in English.

C always has a "K" sound as in "car."

Ch always has a "K" sound as in "chorus."

G always has a hard "G" sound as in "get."

Gu is pronounced "Gw" when it comes after an "n," as it is in English.

I is a consonant pronounced like "Y" when it is the first letter in a word and it is followed by a vowel. The common Latin word iam (now) is pronounced "YAHM."

Qu is pronounced "Kw," as it is in English.

R can be rolled in a sort of Scottish burr.

S   always has a hissing sound as in "m<u>oose</u>" or "<u>s</u>oda," and some
      very common word endings sound like this: <u>as</u> = "demi-
      ta<u>sse</u>"; <u>es</u> = "<u>ace</u>"; <u>is</u> = "<u>geese</u>"; <u>os</u> = "verb<u>ose</u>"; and <u>us</u> =
      "w<u>uss</u>."

T   always has a hard "T" sound as in "<u>t</u>ar." In Latin, the word
      "ratio" is pronounced "RAH-tee-oh."

V   is always pronounced as if it were a "W." What Caesar (KYE-
      sahr) said after he defeated somebody or other *(veni, vidi,
      vici)* sounded as if he had just conquered Hawaii: WAY-nee,
      WEE-dee, WEE-kee.*

X   is always pronounced "Ks."

J, W, and Y don't exist in Latin.

III SYLLABLES

It looks like a tricky language, but you'll get the hang of it
      pretty quickly.

* *Lingua speciem involutam praebet, sed sat cito eam*
      comprehendes.
   LEEN-gwah SPAY-kee-ehm inn-woh-LOO-tahm PRYE-bayt,
   SEDD SAHT KEE-toh AY-ahm kohm-pray-HAYN-dace.

Latin words are divided into syllables in the same way that English
words are, but in Latin every vowel or dipthong is a syllable, and
every syllable is pronounced separately. If there are two vowels
together, and they are not AE, AU, or OE, both vowels are pronounced individually. So, for example, <u>prae</u>bat = "PRYE-baht" (ae
is a dipthong); <u>spec</u>iem = "SPAY-kee-ehm"; and <u>eam</u> = "AY-
ahm."

* If you took Latin in a parochial school, you were probably taught to
pronounce the letter "V" like the English "V," the dipthong "ae" like
"sund<u>ae</u>", and Caesar like "CHAY-sahr." If you do this, you are going to
take <u>s</u>ome flak from Latin purists, classics snobs, and other assorted lingo
bores, but on the other hand, you're going to get a much better table in the
Vatican restaurant.

IV STRESS

And remember, there aren't any Romans around to correct
your pronunciation.
- *Atque memento, nulli adsunt Romanorum qui locutionem tuam
corrigant.*
AHT-kway may-MAYN-toh, NOO-lee AHD-soont Roh-mah-
NOH-ruhm KWEE loh-koo-tee-OH-nehm TOO-ahm KOH-
ree-gahnt.

If a word has two syllables, put the stress on the first one. If it has
more than two, put the stress on the second-to-last syllable unless
both the second-to-last syllable and the last syllable are vowels.
When that happens, shift the stress back one syllable earlier.

So, for example, locutionem = "loh-koo-tee-OH-nehm," but locutio = "loh-KOO-tee-oh."

If the second-to-last syllable has an "i" in it and doesn't end in
a consonant, the stress is usually moved back one syllable. So, for
example, corrigant = "KOHR-ree-gahnt" and dificilissimum =
"dee-fee-kee-LEESE-ee-muhm." For the same reason, the very common word aliqui (any) is pronounced "AH-lee-kwee."

I.
CONVERSATIONAL LATIN
Lingua Latina Conlocutioni

Cocktail Party Chitchat

Hot enough for you?
- *Satine caloris tibi est!*

Run into much traffic on the way over?
- *Turbane magna vehiculorum obviam erat tibi venienti huc!*

What do you think I paid for this watch?
- *Quanto putas mihi stare hoc horologium manuale!*

You know what I think? I think . . .
- *Visne scire quod credam! Credo . . .*

> . . . that all wrestling is fixed.
> . . . *luctationes omnes praestitutas esse.*

> . . . that flying saucers are real.
> . . . *orbes volantes exstare.*

> . . . that Elvis is still alive.
> . . . *Elvem ipsum etiam vivere.*

> . . . that the weather has been altered by rocket launches.
> . . . *missiones turrium flammearum statum caeli mutavisse.*

> . . . that no one's barbecue sauce is better than mine.
> . . . *condimentum pro carne in veribus cocta nullius praestare ei mei.*

CONVERSATION FILLERS

Is that so?
- *Ain tu?*

Really?
- *Vero?*

You don't say!
- *Dic! Itane est?*

You can say that again!
- *Illud iterum dicere potes!*

You know what they say . . .
- *Scis quod dicunt . . .*

      . . . here today, gone tomorrow.
      . . . *hodie adsit, cras absit.*

      . . . seen one, seen them all.
      . . . *uno viso, omnia visa sunt.*

      . . . what goes around, comes around.
      . . . *id quod circumiret, circumveniat.*

      . . . *que sera, sera.*
      . . . *quod fiat, fiat.*

CONVERSATION ENDERS

God, look at the time! My wife will kill me!
- *Di! Ecce hora! Uxor mea me necabit!*

Excuse me. I've got to see a man about a dog.
- *Mihi ignosce. Cum homine de cane debeo congredi.*

Darn! There goes my beeper!
- *Heu! Tintinnuntius meus sonat!*

I'm outta here.
- *Abeo.*

Have a nice day.
- *Die dulci fruere.*

PITHY LATIN EXPRESSIONS TO USE IN ENGLISH

Ipso facto
- By that very fact

Nullo modo
- No way

Labra lege.
- Read my lips.

Pactum factum
- A done deal

Fors fortis
- Fat chance

Casu consulto
- Accidentally on purpose

Raptus regaliter
- Royally screwed

Totus anctus
- In a world of hurt

Utinam
- Hopefully

II.
INFORMATIONAL LATIN

Lingua Latina Nuntiis

Latin Signs for Our Times

CAVE CANEM
- BEWARE OF DOG

NOLI PERTURBARE
- DO NOT DISTURB

NOLI INTRARE
- KEEP OUT

OPORTET MINISTROS MANUS LAVARE ANTEQUAM LATRINAM RELINQUENT
- EMPLOYEES MUST WASH HANDS BEFORE LEAVING RESTROOM

BARBARI! IN HOC CURRU NULLA ARCA SONORUM ADSIT!
- NO RADIO!

TIBI GRATIAS AGIMUS QUOD NIHIL FUMAS
- THANK YOU FOR NOT SMOKING

SI HOC SIGNUM LEGERE POTES, OPERIS BONI IN REBUS LATINIS ALACRIBUS ET FRUCTUOSIS POTIRI POTES!
- IF YOU CAN READ THIS SIGN, YOU CAN GET A GOOD JOB IN THE FAST-PACED, HIGH-PAYING WORLD OF LATIN!

Latin Bumper Stickers for Your Chariot

FRENA PRO FERIS TENEO
- I BRAKE FOR ANIMALS

BALAENAE NOBIS CONSERVANDAE SUNT
- SAVE THE WHALES

SONA SI LATINE LOQUERIS
- HONK IF YOU SPEAK LATIN

CUM CATAPULTAE PROSCRIPTAE ERUNT TUM SOLI PROSCRIPTI CATAPULTAS HABEBUNT
- WHEN CATAPULTS ARE OUTLAWED, ONLY OUTLAWS WILL HAVE CATAPULTS

SI HOC ADFIXUM IN OBICE LEGERE POTES, ET LIBERALITER EDUCATUS ET NIMIS PROPINQUUS ADES
- IF YOU CAN READ THIS BUMPER STICKER, YOU ARE BOTH VERY WELL EDUCATED AND MUCH TOO CLOSE

Vanitas Plates

INCITATUS
- SPEED DEMON

VAGANS
- CRUISING

LITORALIS
- BEACH BUM

MANNUS
- MUSTANG

FRACTUM
- JALOPY

NITIDUS
- SNAZZY

URSUS
- BEAR

AMO VI-UM
- I LOVE SEX

TURBO
- TURBO

Latin as a Computer Language

Why won't you print out?
- *Cur ullum imprimere non vis!*

Don't you dare erase my hard disk!
- *Ne auderis delere orbem rigidum meum!*

I did not commit a fatal error!
- *Non erravi perniciose!*

Garbage in, garbage out.
- *Purgamentum init, exit purgamentum.*

An All-Purpose Personal Ad

Attractive and intelligent man/woman wishes to meet a Latin speaker of the opposite sex. Please—no pig Latin!

Vir/mulier iucundus/iucunda intellegensque vult obviam convenire alicui sexus adversi qui lingua Latina utitur. Amabo—nihil loquelae Latinae suillae!

An All-Purpose Letter

Dear Sir:
I have received your letter and I will give the matter to which you referred my promptest and fullest attention.

Best wishes,

Dominus meus:
Epistulam tuam accepi et rei cuius mentionem ibi fecisti animadversionem meam promptissimam plenissimamque dabo.

Semper vale et salve,

An All-Purpose Postcard Message

Having a wonderful time. I wish you were here. Or should it be, I should wish you had been here? Or maybe, I should have been wishing that you had been here? Or, I did wish you to have been here?

Best,

Tempus dulcissime oblecto. Volo ut mecum adsis. Aut debetne dicere, Velim ut mecum aderis? Aut fortasse, Vellem ut mecum adfueris? Aut, Volui te mecum adfuisse?

Optationes optimas ad te,

An All-Purpose Answering-Machine Message

Hello. No one can come to the phone right now to take your call, but you can leave a message if you want by speaking as soon as you hear the beep. Remember to wait for the beep. Bye.

Salve. Nemo nunc ipsum advenire ad longelocutum ad vocem tuam accipiendam potest, sed possis si velis nuntiam tradere dicendo simul ac sonitum audiveris. Memento sonitu praestolare. Ave.

An All-Purpose Telephone Prank

Hello, is this the supermarket? Do you have Janitor in a Drum and Mr. Clean in a bottle? You do? Well, let them out! Ha ha ha!

Dic, estne magnimercatus? Estne vobis Ianitor in Cupa et Magister Purus in ampulla? Sicine? Bene, eos emitte! Hae hae hae!

An All-Purpose Stick-up Note

I have a catapult. Give me all the money, or I will fling an enormous rock at your head.

Catapultam habeo. Nisi pecuniam omnem mihi dabis, ad caput tuum saxum immane mittam.

NEGOTIATING IN LATIN

I'd like to cut a deal.
- *Volo pactum facere.*

Now this isn't carved in stone.
- *Nunc hoc in marmore non est incisum.*

This is just a ballpark figure.
- *Hic est numerus, plus aut minus.*

I'm thinking out loud.
- *Clara voce cogito.*

This is all blue sky.
- *Totum de caelo caeruleo venit.*

I think we're on the same wavelength.
- *Credo nos in fluctu eodem esse.*

SWEETENING THE DEAL

Can you put more money on the table?
• *Potesne plus pecuniae in mensa ponere?*

Let's look at the bottom line.
• *Summam scrutemur.*

Is that your best offer?
• *Num ista condicio optima est?*

Can't you sharpen up your pencil a little on this?
• *Nonne potes stilum tuum in hac re paulum acuere?*

If you can't go any higher, the deal is off.
• *Si plus offerre non potes, pactum ruptum est.*

PLAYING HARDBALL

We're back to square one.
• *In carceribus denuo adsumus.*

I'm wasting my time.
• *Tempus meum tero.*

That's the deal. Take it or leave it.
• *Ecce pactum. Id cape aut id relinque.*

You're not the only game in town.
• *In oppido lusor solus non es.*

Well, you win some, you lose some.
• *Modo vincis, modo vinceris.*

HIDDEN INSULTS

LATIN	WHAT YOU SAY IT MEANS	WHAT IT REALLY MEANS
Podex perfectus es.	You did a terrific job.	You are a total asshole.
De stella Martis vere venisti.	That's a truly remarkable insight.	You are definitely from Mars.
Stercorem pro cerebro habes.	That's certainly food for thought.	You have shit for brains.
Caput tuum in ano est.	You hit the nail right on the head.	You have your head up your ass.
Futue te ipsum et caballum tuum.	I've really got to take my hat off to you.	Screw you and the horse you rode in on.

USEFUL BUSINESS EXPRESSIONS

Take the bull by the horns.
- *Taurum per cornua prehende.*

It comes with the territory.
- *Cum tractu traducto.*

Give me a little feedback.
- *Dic mihi paulum quod sentis.*

If it ain't broke, don't fix it.
- *Si fractum non sit, noli id reficere.*

Get your ducks in a row.
- *Anates tuas in acie instrue.*

The ball is in your court.
- *Pila in area tua est.*

I'm up the creek without a paddle.
- *In rivo fimi sine remo sum.*

It ain't over until it's over.
- *Id imperfectum manet dum confectum erit.*

Making a Cold Call

I'd like to bounce something off you.
- *Aliquo te volo petere.*

You seem like someone who knows a good thing when he
sees it.
- *Tute videris esse qui noscat rem bonam cum videat.*

It's a once-in-a-lifetime opportunity.
- *Occasio rarissima est.*

I'm sorry we couldn't do business.
- *Stercorem pro cerebro habes.**

* See Hidden Insults, p. 19

THE UNA-MINUTIA MANAGER

Take a letter.
- *Scribe.*

Xerox[R] this.
- *Huius Xerographiam[P] fac.*

Hold my calls.
- *Fac ut nemo me vocet.*

I don't get headaches. I give them.
- *Dolores capitis non fero. Eos do.*

The buck stops here.
- *Denarius hic sistit.*

There's no free lunch.
- *Nulla mensa sine impensa.*

You're fired.
- *Ego te demitto.*

MOGUL JARGON

Let's take a meeting.
- *Congressum faciamus.*

Have your people talk to my people.
- *Tuos iube meis dicere.*

What's the net-net on this?
- *Quid in re reditum residuum reliquumque restat?*

It's the standard deal.
- *Conventum consuetum est.*

Baby, sweetheart, would I lie to you?
- *Amicule, deliciae, num is sum qui mentiar tibi?*

Let's cut to the chase.
- *Ad venatum vadamus.*

Don't pass on this!
- *Noli hoc praeterire!*

Give me a green light!
- *Da mihi lumen viride!*

You're beautiful!
- *Pulcher es!*

Let's have lunch, really!
- *Prandeamus, vere!*

IV.
RECREATIONAL LATIN

Lingua Latina Oblectamentis

At the Football Stadium

These are great seats, aren't they?
- *Sedilia haec, nonne praestant?*

First and ten, do it again! Touchdown!
- *Primum et decem est, rursum agendum est! Detractum!*

God, these halftime shows are boring.
- *Hercle, ludicra haec inter dimidia muneris intercedentia insulsa sunt.*

At the Ball Park

I hate Astroturf.
- *Gramen artificiosum odi.*

The designated-hitter rule has got to go.
- *Lex clavatoris designati rescindenda est.*

The best baseball stadium is still Fenway Park.
- *Stadium sedipilae optimum Saeptum Paludosum etiamnunc est.*

CHEERING FOR YOUR TEAM

Let's go . . .
- *Eamus, O . . .*

AMERICAN LEAGUE/EAST

Orioles	*Icteri Galbuli*
Yankees	*Ianqui*
Blue Jays	*Cyanocittae Cristatae*
Brewers	*Fermentatores*
Red Sox	*Tibialia Rubentia*
Indians	*Indi*
Tigers	*Tigres*

AMERICAN LEAGUE/WEST

A's	*Athletici*
Angels	*Angeli*
Royals	*Regii*
Rangers	*Equites*
Twins	*Gemini*
Mariners	*Nautae*
White Sox	*Tibialia Alba*

NATIONAL LEAGUE/EAST

Expos	*Expositiones*
Mets	*Metropolitae*
Cubs	*Catuli*
Cardinals	*Cardinales*
Pirates	*Piratae*
Phillies	*Philadelphii*

Giants	*Gigantes*
Astros	*Astrotholi Incolae*
Reds	*Rubri*
Dodgers	*Elusores*
Padres	*Patri*
Braves	*Fortes*

AT A HOCKEY GAME

Hockey fans are real animals.
• *Fautores ludi glacialis Borei feri meri sunt.*

Here comes the Zamboni.
• *Huc accedit Zambonis.*

AT THE POKER TABLE

Read 'em and weep.
• *Lege atque lacrima.*

This isn't a hand, it's a foot.
• *Hoc non manus sed pes est.*

On the Golf Course

I'm going to take a Mulligan.
- *Alterum ictum faciam.*

We're playing winter rules, aren't we?
- *Nonne lege hiemali ludimus?*

This is a gimme, isn't it?
- *Nonne hoc mihi datur?*

Isn't that lucky! My ball just rolled out of the rough and onto the fairway!
- *Fortunatus sum! Pila mea de gramine horrido modo in pratum lene recta volvit!*

On the Tennis Court

It's just out!
- *Paulo praeter regionem est!*

A little wide!
- *Minime latum!*

It was just a hair long!
- *Longius capillo fuit!*

It's out by an inch!
- *Una uncia abest!*

On the Slopes

Boy, I hate lift lines.
- *Heu, odi manere in agmine pro sellis volatilibus.*

Watch where you're going, you jerk!
- *Observa quo vadis, cinaede!*

Avalanche!
- *Lapsus nivium!*

Let's get in the hot tub!
- *In thermulas intremus!*

At the Beach

Look at the hooters on that one.
- *Ecce illa mammeata.*

Let's build a sand Forum.
- *Forum harenae aedificemus.*

Do you want a frosty one?
- *Visne frigidum?*

What's that in the water?
- *Quid est illud in aqua?*

Shark! Shark!
- *Pistrix! Pistrix!*

On a Yacht

What happens if I pull this rope?
- *Quid fiat si hoc rudentem vellam?*

Can I drive?
- *Licetne mihi gubernare?*

Is there supposed to be a lot of water down here?
- *Debetne multum aquae subter esse?*

All of a sudden I'm not feeling so good.
- *Subito minime valeo.*

At the Spa

There is something wrong with this scale.
- *Haec trutina errat.*

Was your masseur trained in East Germany?
- *Tractatorne in Germania Orientali doctus est?*

It's on a plate, it must be food.
- *In catillo est, cibus esse debet.*

Is there an alcoholic beverage made from oat bran?
- *Estne ebriamen de furfure avenaceo factum?*

THINGS TO SAY TO YOUR LAWYER

Listen, would you repeat everything you just told me, only this time say it in English.
- *Heu, modo itera omnia quae mihi nunc nuper narravisti, sed nunc Anglice.*

You charge how much an hour?
- *Quantum in una hora imputas?*

THINGS TO SAY TO YOUR ACCOUNTANT

This amount here, is that what I made or what I owe?
- *Haec summa, estne quod merui aut quod debeo?*

Where do I sign?
- *Ubi signo?*

THINGS TO SAY TO THE IRS AGENT

Unfortunately, I can't find those particular documents.
- *Eheu, litteras istas reperire non possum.*

I know why the numbers don't agree! I use Roman numerals!
- *Scio cur summae inter se dissentiant! Numeris Romanis utor!*

THINGS TO SAY TO YOUR BANKER

I don't want a toaster.
- *Furnulum pani nolo.*

I can't be overdrawn.
- *Fieri non potest ut ratio mea deficiat.*

THINGS TO SAY TO YOUR STOCKBROKER

Just what exactly is a pork belly?
- *Quidnam est sterilicula?*

I thought the idea was to buy low and sell high.
- *Credidi pretio parvo emere et magno vendere tibi in animo fuisse.*

Are you telling me that sunspots caused the market crash?
- *Dicisne mihi maculas in sole mercatum labi fecisse?*

Things to Say to Your Dentist

This isn't going to hurt, is it?
- *Num mihi dolebit hoc?*

Something important came up, so I'll have to cancel my appointment.
- *Quadam re magna facta constitutum meum mihi deponendum est.*

Things to Say to Your Psychiatrist

Sometimes I get this urge to conquer large parts of Europe.
- *Interdum feror cupidine partium magnarum Europae vincendarum.*

I think some people in togas are plotting against me.
- *Sentio aliquos togatos contra me conspirare.*

I have this compulsion to speak Latin.
- *Latine loqui coactus sum.*

What has my mother got to do with it?
- *Quid agitur de matre mea?*

THINGS TO SAY TO A TEENAGER

Really rad, dude!
- *Radicitus, comes!*

What's happening?
- *Quid fit?*

THINGS TO SAY TO AN OBNOXIOUS CHILD

In the good old days, children like you were left to perish on windswept crags.
- *Antiquis temporibus, nati tibi similes in rupibus ventosissimis exponebantur ad necem.*

I'm rubber, you're glue, bounces off me, sticks to you!
- *Flexilis sum, gluten es, me resilit, ad te haeret!*

THINGS TO SAY TO A MOVIE STAR

You look shorter and older in person.
- *Videris humilior seniorque coram.*

Can I have your autograph?
- *Licetne tibi mihi dare tuam subscriptionem?*

Things to Say to the Hoi Polloi

I do not have any spare change.
- *Est mihi nullus nummus superfluus.*

I gave at the office.
- *In tabulario donationem feci.*

I do not wish to "check it out."
- *Nolo id "perscrutari."*

I'm not interested in your dopey religious cult.
- *Nihil curo de ista tua stulta superstitione.*

If Caesar were alive, you'd be chained to an oar.
- *Caesar si viveret, ad remum dareris.*

Things to Say to a Malfunctioning Soft-Drink Machine

You infernal machine! Give me a beverage or give me back my money!
- *Machina improba! Vel mihi ede potum vel mihi redde nummos meos!*

Embarrassing Situations Are Less Embarrassing in Latin

I'd like to buy some condoms.
- *Volo comparare nonnulla tegumembra.*

I didn't expect you home so soon!
- *Non sperabam te domum tam cito revenire!*

I don't know how that got into my pocket.
- *Nescio quomodo illud in sinum meum intraverit.*

Of course I know what day today is! I just can't remember the English word for it.
- *Scilicet scio quid sit hodiernus dies! Modo ei non possum meminisse verbum Anglicum.*

Oh! I was just looking to see whether you had any Kleenex here among these papers on your desk.
- *O! Conabar cognoscere num tibi adsit Nascida in mensa tua inter haec scripta.*

Do you by any chance happen to own a large, yellowish, very flat cat?
- *Estne tibi forte magna feles fulva et planissima!*

BALD-FACED LIES ARE LESS BALD-FACED IN LATIN

The check is in the mail.
- *Perscriptio in manibus tabellariorum est.*

I have nothing to declare.
- *Nihil declaro.*

I don't know what you're talking about.
- *Nescio quid dicas.*

It was that way when I got here.
- *Ita erat quando hic adveni.*

There's no one here by that name.
- *Nemo hic adest illius nominis.*

Don't call me, I'll call you.
- *Noli me vocare, ego te vocabo.*

FLATTERY SOUNDS MORE SINCERE IN LATIN

Have you lost weight?
- *Nonne macescis?*

You haven't aged a bit!
- *Minime senuisti!*

It looks great on you!
- *Id tibi praebet speciem lepidissimam!*

A wig? I never would have guessed!
- *Capillamentum? Haudquaquam conieci esse!*

Intimate Subjects Are Easier to Broach in Latin

Your fly is open.
- *Braccae tuae aperiuntur.*

Your slip is showing.
- *Subucula tua apparet.*

You have a big piece of spinach on your front teeth.
- *In dentibus anticis frustum magnum spinaciae habes.*

You've been misusing the subjunctive.
- *Abutebaris modo subjunctivo.*

Self-Assertiveness Is Simpler in Latin

Hey, we're all in line here!
- *Heus, hic nos omnes in agmine sunt!*

No cutting in!
- *Noli inferre se in agmen!*

No, excuse me, I believe *I'm* next.
- *Non, mihi ignosce, credo me insequentem esse.*

You're from New York, aren't you?
- *Nonne de Novo Eboraco venis?*

Threats Carry More Weight in Latin

Watch out—you might end up divided into three parts, like Gaul.
- *Prospice tibi—ut Gallia, tu quoque in tres partes dividaris.*

People will soon be referring to you in the past pluperfect tense.
- *In tempore praeterito plus quam perfecto de te mox dicent.*

If I were you, I wouldn't walk in front of any catapults.
- *Cave ne ante ullas catapultas ambules.*

FIGHTING WORDS ARE SAFER IN LATIN

What did you call me?
- *Quid me appellavisti?*

Yeah, I'm talking to you.
- *Ita, te adloquor.*

You want to repeat that?
- *Visne illud iterare?*

A comedian, huh?
- *Ita vero, esne comoedus?*

Oh yeah? Your mother!
- *Itane? Tua mater!*

You want to make something of it?
- *Visne aliquid de illo facere?*

You and whose army?
- *Tutene? Atque cuius exercitus?*

Let's step outside.
- *Foras gradiamur.*

Well, if you don't understand plain Latin, I'm not going to dirty my hands on you.
- *Bene, cum Latine nescias, nolo manus meas in te maculare.*

EXCUSES SOUND MORE BELIEVABLE IN LATIN

My dog ate it.
- *Canis meus id comedit.*

The cleaning lady threw it away.
- *Ancilla id abiecit.*

It fell into the shredder.
- *Id in machinam schidarum scindendarum incedit.*

I did call. Maybe your answering machine is broken.
- *Sane ego te vocavi. Forsitan capedictum tuum desit.*

My watch stopped.
- *Horologium manuale meum stitit.*

My car wouldn't start.
- *Currus meus se movere noluit.*

I was kidnapped by aliens. What year is it?
- *Hostes alienigeni me abduxerunt. Qui annus est?*

B.S. Is More Convincing in Latin

I'm glad you asked me that.
- *Gaudeo te illud de me rogavisse.*

I'll put all my cards on the table.
- *Chartas meas omnes in tabulam ponam.*

You know, I'm your biggest fan.
- *Edepol, fautor tuus maximus sum.*

I'm only thinking of what's best for you.
- *Modo cogito quid prosit rebus tuis.*

Believe me, this hurts me more than it hurts you.
- *Mihi crede, hoc mihi magis quam tibi nocet.*

Latin Medical Names for Nonexistent But Useful Diseases

Impedimentum memoriae
- (A mental block that makes it hard for you to remember names)

Inopia celeritatis
- (A mild dyslexia that makes it impossible to arrive on time)

Dolor anteprandialis
- (A gastric problem that occasionally makes you cancel a lunch)

Morbus irrigationis
- (A rare disease aggravated by watering friends' plants)

Taedium pellucidorum
- (An eye condition that keeps you from looking at people's slides)

An All-Purpose Evasion of a Request for a Latin Translation

You can't say that in Latin.
- *Illud Latine dici non potest.*

An All-Purpose Phony Translation of a Latin Inscription

"Having done these things, they made the sacrifices prescribed by custom lest they be found lacking in filial piety."

At the Theater

If you want good tickets, you've got to go to a scalper.
- *Si desideras tesseras bonas tibi opus est ad sectorem ire.*

You know, we really ought to go to the theater more often.
- *Pol, ad spectaculum saepius nobis eundum est.*

Fire!
- *Flamma!*

At a Concert

What time do you think we'll be out of here?
- *Quo tempore credis nos exituros?*

Is it over? Do I applaud now?
- *Estne confectum? Nuncine applaudo?*

At a Literary Gathering

Seen any good movies lately?
- *Vidistine nuper imagines moventes bonas?*

How about those Forty-Niners?
- *Quid sentis de Undequinquagintis?*

At a Poetry Reading

It doesn't rhyme.
- *Nullo metro compositum est.*

I don't care. If it doesn't rhyme, it isn't a poem.
- *Non curo. Si metrum non habet, non est poema.*

At an Art Exhibition

You call this art? A two-year-old could do better.
- *Dicisne hoc opus artem esse? Quivis infans rem meliorem facere potest.*

I don't know much about art, but I know what I like.
- *Cum Musis deditus non sim, nosco quod amo.*

At the Vatican

Know where I can get a cup of coffee around here?
- *Scisne ubi pocillum coffeae apud hanc locum possim capere?*

Is this the way to the Sistine Chapel?
- *Ducitne haec via ad Capellam Sextinam?*

Is it all right if I use a flash in here?
- *Licetne mihi hic fulgure uteri?*

Now *that's* a ceiling!
- *Ecce lacunar mirum!*

Is this the only gift shop?
- *Haecine taberna munusculorum unica est?*

Excuse me, can you recommend a good restaurant nearby?
- *Nisi molestum est, potesne mihi recommendare popinam bonam vicinam?*

Where can I get a hat like that?
- *Ubi possum potiri petasi similis isti?*

At the Movies

This is a remake of a French film.
- *Haec imago movens ex pristina Gallicana recreata est.*

The sequel is never as good as the original.
- *Sequella numquam tam bona est quam origo.*

Look out, there's some crud on this seat.
- *Cave, aliquod squaloris est in hac sede.*

Timeless Lines from the Movies

Make my day.
- *Fac ut gaudeam.*

Round up the usual suspects.
- *Conlige suspectos semper habitos.*

You know, Toto, I have a feeling we're not in Kansas anymore.
- *Certe, Toto, sentio nos in Kansate non iam adesse.*

Frankly, my dear, I don't give a damn.
- *Re vera, cara mea, mea nil refert.*

All Music Is Classical Music in Latin

My favorite group is . . .
- *Caterva carissima mea est . . .*

The Beatles
Cimictus

The Rolling Stones
Lapides Provolventes

The Grateful Dead
Mortui Grati

The Beach Boys
Pueri Litoris

The Temptations
Inlecebrae

The Who
Ille Quis

The Monkees
Simitatores

Country Joe and the Fish
Iosephus Agrestis Piscesque

ALL TV IS EDUCATIONAL TV IN LATIN

My favorite show is . . .
* *Spectaculum carissimum est . . .*

Gilligan's Island
Insula Gilliganis

Hollywood Squares
Quadrata Iliceti

The Love Boat
Navis Amoris

Leave It to Beaver
Id Castori Concedite

Mission: Impossible
Opus: Quod Fieri Non Potest

Hawaii Five-O
Hawaii Quinque-Nil

The Gong Show
Spectaculum Tintinnabuli

The Price Is Right
Pretium Iustum Est

Jeopardy
Periculum

Wheel of Fortune
Rota Fortunae

Diff'rent Strokes
Ictus Diff'rentes

Happy Days
Dies Felices

The Young and the Restless
Iuvenes Inquietesque

Divorce Court
Curia Divortiorum

The Flintstones
Illi Silices

The Twilight Zone
Zona Crepusculi

In a Bar

I'll have . . .
- *Da mihi sis . . .*

> . . . a light beer.
> . . . *cerevisiam dilutam.*

> . . . a glass of white wine.
> . . . *poculum vini albi.*

> . . . a martini.
> . . . *spiculum argenteum.*

> . . . a fog cutter.
> . . . *quod nebulam dissipat.*

I'll drink to that!
- *Hoc ei propinabo!*

Bartender! Another round!
- *Caupo! Etiamnunc!*

Cheers!
- *Propino tibi salutem!*

At a WASP Country Club

That is the largest drink I have ever seen.
- *Illa potio maxima est a me visa.*

I think several of the people here are dead.
- *Credo nonnullos hic mortuos esse.*

Those green pants go so well with that pink shirt and the plaid jacket!
- *Braccae illae virides cum subucula rosea et tunica Caledonia—quam eleganter concinnatur!*

I can't understand what you are saying. Are your jaws wired together?
- *Verba tua intellegere non possum. Filone ferreo maxillae tuae iunctae sunt?*

At a Hip Disco

Do you want to dance? I know the Funky Broadway.
- *Visne saltare? Viam Latam Fungosam scio.*

How do you get your hair to do that?
- *Quomodo cogis comas tuas sic videri?*

AT A BIRTHDAY PARTY

Happy birthday!
- *Tibi diem natalem felicem!*

Here's a pinch to grow an inch!
- *Te vellico ut uncia crescas!*

Speech! Speech!
- *Ora! Ora!*

AT A FAMILY REUNION

Put on a little weight, haven't you?
- *Nonne aliquantulum pinguescis?*

Is that a gray hair?
- *Illaecine canities?*

Honey/buster, when are you going to get married?
- *Mellita/comes, quando aliquem/aliquam in matrimonium accipies/duces?*

You're not going to get a divorce, are you?
- *Num est tibi in animo divortium facere?*

Face it, you're stuck in a dead-end job.
- *Aspice, officio fungeris sine spe honoris amplioris.*

Say, you sure are drinking a lot.
- *Re vera, potas bene.*

Isn't it great to have the whole family together?
- *Nonne dulce est familiam totam in unum locum cogere?*

At Your High School Reunion

Oh! Was I speaking Latin again?
- *Vah! Denuone Latine loquebar?*

Silly me. Sometimes it just sort of slips out.
- *Me ineptum. Interdum modo elabitur.*

Talking to Pets

Polly want a cracker?
- *Pulle! Visne frustum?*

Sit! Roll over! You see, he understands Latin.
- *Sede! Volve! Ecce, Latine scit.*

Bad kitty! Why don't you use the cat box? I put new litter in it.
- *Feles mala! Cur cista non uteris? Stramentum novum in ea posui.*

Useful Curses

May barbarians invade your personal space!
- *Utinam barbari spatium proprium tuum invadant!*

May conspirators assassinate you in the mall!
- *Utinam coniurati te in foro interficiant!*

May faulty logic undermine your entire philosophy!
- *Utinam logica falsa tuam philosophiam totam suffodiant!*

May you always misuse the subjunctive!
- *Utinam modo subiunctivo semper male utaris!*

BIOLOGICAL TERMS OF ENDEARMENT

Homo sapiens
- A human being

Fiber fervidus
- An eager beaver

Cuniculus inscius
- A dumb bunny

Pavo absolutus
- A total turkey

Lacertus atrioli
- A lounge lizard

Fera festiva
- A party animal

Radix lecti
- A couch potato

STARTING A RELATIONSHIP

Do you come here often?
- *Frequentasne hunc locum?*

Haven't we met somewhere before?
- *Nonne alicubi prius convenimus?*

What's your sign?
- *Quo signo nata es?*

You strike me as a very deep person.
- *Apparet te habere ingenium profundum.*

I feel that I already know you.
- *Sentio me iam te novisse.*

I think fate brought us together.
- *Credo fatum nos coegisse.*

Your place or mine?
- *Apudne te vel me?*

Having a Relationship

You know, the Romans invented the art of love.
- *Romani quidem artem amatoriam invenerunt.*

A little more up and to the right.
- *Paululum sursum et dextrorsum.*

Oh! More! Go on! Yes! Ooh! Ummm!
- *O! Plus! Perge! Aio! Hui! Hem!*

Ending the Relationship

Let's not rush into anything.
- *In ullam rem ne properemus.*

I'm not ready to make a commitment.
- *Non sum paratus me committere.*

I'm not sure we're right for each other.
- *Nescio num alius idoneus alii sit.*

I hope we'll still be friends.
- *Spero nos familiares mansuros.*

I guess fate wanted us to part.
- *Suspicor fatum nos voluisse diversos.*

IN A FAST-FOOD RESTAURANT

I'll have . . .
* *Da mihi sis . . .*

   . . . a hamburger, French fries, and a thick shake.
   . . . *bubulae frustum assae, solana tuberosa in modo*
      Gallico fricta ac quassum lactatum coagulatum
      crassum.

   . . . a bucket of fried chicken.
   . . . *hamam pulli tosti.*

   . . . a pizza with everything on it.
   . . . *crustum Etruscum cum omnibus in eo.*

IN A CHAIN THEME RESTAURANT

I want the Buffalo chicken wings.
* *Alas gallinaceas de urbe Bovis volo.*

The waitress drew a smiley face on my check.
* *Ancilla in computatione faciem subridentem pinxit.*

AT A PRETENTIOUS RESTAURANT

Frankly, I think the chef put too much thyme in the sauce.
- *Ut vere dicam, credo coquum nimium thymi in liquamen mississe.*

Look at the size of that pepper mill.
- *Ecce magnitudinem illae molae piperi.*

It's a nice little wine, but it lacks character and depth.
- *Vinum bellum iucundumque est, sed animo corporeque caret.*

IN A CHINESE RESTAURANT

Please, no MSG.
- *Parce, sodes, glutamato monosodio.*

Do you have "flied lice?" Ha ha ha.
- *Habesne "olyzam flictam?" Hae hae hae.*

At the Stop 'n' Shop

Look! . . .
- *Ecce!* . . .

. . . Jelly beans
. . . *Fabae suaves*

. . . Gummy Bears
. . . *Ursuli Gummi*

. . . Bubble gum
. . . *Manducabulla*

. . . Mars Bars
. . . *Lateres Martiales*

. . . Milky Ways
. . . *Viae Lacteae*

. . . Moon Pies
. . . *Crusta Lunares*

. . . Pretzels
. . . *Nodi salsi*

. . . Potato chips
. . . *Assulae solanorum tuberosorum*

. . . Coca-Cola
. . . *Cola-Coca*

. . . Cheez Whiz
. . . *Caseus Velox*

. . . Twinkies
. . . *Scintillae*

. . . Tinfoil
. . . *Bractea stannea*

. . . Glad Bags
. . . *Sacci Laeti*

. . . Aspirin
. . . *Pilulae acetylsalicylicae*

THINGS TO SAY WHILE BARBECUING

Take a look at those steaks!
- *Contemplare carunculas illas!*

You've really got to soak the charcoal with fuel.
- *Necesse est carbonem igne Graeco madefacere.*

The mosquitoes are murder tonight!
- *Culices pessimi hac nocte sunt!*

Ever noticed how wherever you stand, the smoke goes right
into your face?
- *Animadvertistine, ubicumque stes, fumum recta in faciem ferri?*

Come and get it!
- *Venite ac capite!*

A ROMAN RECIPE

1. Get 1,000 larks.
2. Remove their tongues and set aside.
3. Discard the larks.
4. Put the tongues in a pan with a little oil and sauté quickly.
5. Transfer to a hot platter. Serves four.

I. *Alaudarum* M *cape.*
II. *Linguas exseca et sepone.*
III. *Alaudas abice.*
IV. *Linguas mitte in sartaginem cum paulo olei et frige cito.*
V. *Eas traice ad patellam calidam. Quattuor sufficit.*

XI.
FAMILIAL LATIN
Lingua Latina Domestica

DOMESTIC DISCOURSE

Honey, I'm home.
- *Mellita, domi adsum.*

Sheesh, what a day!
- *Mehercle, qui dies!*

You did what to the car?
- *Quid carrus passus est?*

You paid how much for that dress?
- *Quantum illae stolae pependisti?*

Something's burning.
- *Aliquid ardet.*

Oh, no, it's the roast, and the boss is coming to dinner!
- *Vae, ardet assa bubula atque patronus ad cenam veniet!*

MINOR MISUNDERSTANDINGS

Shopping list? What shopping list?
* *Libellus comparandorum! Qui libellus comparandorum!*

I thought you were going to pick up the kids.
* *Credidi te liberos colligere.*

Don't ask me where the keys are. You had them last.
* *Noli me rogare ubi sint claves. Eas nunc nuper habebas.*

But you told me your mother was coming *next* month!
* *Sed me docuisti matrem tuam* postero *mense venturam esse!*

A call from someone named "Bubbles?" It's a wrong number.
* *Vocatusne de quadam "Bullula" nomine? Numerus falsus est.*

TABLE TALK

My favorite! Tuna-noodle casserole!
* *Mea dilectissima! Farrago thunni!*

What do you say we join the clean-plate club.
* *Nos coniungamus collegio patellae purae.*

You'll eat it and like it, or you'll have it for breakfast
tomorrow.
* *Aut id devorabis amabisque, aut cras prandebis.*

Don't play with your food! Remember the starving
Carthaginians!
* *Noli ludere alimento! Memento Carthaginienses esurientes!*

Laying Down the Law

This report card is a disgrace.
- *Haec renuntatio infamis est.*

Pay attention! I'm speaking to you!
- *Ausculta mihi! Tibi dico!*

You're grounded!
- *Ad domum adligaris!*

No TV for a week!
- *Nullam ultravisionem spectabis per septem dies!*

I'm cutting your allowance in half!
- *Peculium dimidiatum est!*

When I was your age . . .
- *Cum tam iuvenis eram quam nunc es . . .*

> . . . I had a full-time job in a salt mine.
> *. . . in salinis diu laborabam.*

> . . . I won the Nobel Prize for promptness and neatness.
> *. . . Praemium Nobelium celeritatis et munditiae abstuli.*

> . . . I could speak Latin.
> *. . . Latine loqui poteram.*

TOUGH TALK

N-O spells *No!*
- *Verbum non N.O.N. scribitur!*

Nothing doing, and that's final.
- *Haud fiet, et clavo fixum est.*

I don't care what the other parents are doing.
- *Curae mihi non est quod alii parentes faciant.*

I am not being unreasonable.
- *Non sum iniquus.*

All right, we'll ask your mother.
- *Bene, matrem tuam rogabimus.*

Okay, just this once.
- *Ita, semel et solum tibi permissum est.*

DISCUSSING THE BABY-SITTER

I think she's from another planet.
- *Arbitror eam de planeta alia venisse.*

Did her parents drop her off here in a spacecraft?
- *Astroscaphane parentes eam huc portaverunt?*

Maybe she's just a drug addict.
- *Fortasse modo opio addicta est.*

I think I've seen her face on a milk carton or down at the post office.
- *Credo me faciem suam in olla lactis vel in tabulario tabellariorum vidisse.*

IN THE MEN'S DEPARTMENT

This suit looks a little baggy.
- *Vestimentum laxum paululum videtur.*

The lapels are too wide.
- *Fimbriae latiores sunt.*

I don't like this shade.
- *Colorem hunc non diligo.*

Honey, what do you think?
- *Mellilla, quid sentis?*

When will it be ready?
- *Quando praesto fiet?*

ON THE ROAD

We ought to have made that turn.
- *Nos opertuit tunc vertisse.*

Give me the map.
- *Mihi da tabulam.*

Let's ask directions.
- *Aliquem de via consulamus.*

Would you like me to drive?
- *Visne me currum agere?*

I am *not* lost.
- *Neutiquam erro.*

Settle down back there.
- *Sedate vos, posteriores.*

Why didn't you go when you had the chance?
- *Cur non isti mictum ex occasione?*

You'll just have to hold it in.
- *Opus est tibi urinam inhibere.*

Next time you'll take the bus.
- *Carro Canis Cani veharis posthac.*

At a Black-Tie Dinner Party

Let's switch place cards.
- *Chartas loci mutemus.*

Is this the right fork?
- *Hacine furcilla uti decet?*

Wait, that's my bread plate.
- *Sisto, patella panis est mea.*

Do I drink this or stick my fingers in it?
- *Hocine bibo aut in eum digitos insero?*

My dessert is on fire!
- *Mensa secunda mea flagrat!*

At a Wedding

It's not too late to back out!
- *Non serus matrimonium fugias.*

At a Christening

Do you ever worry that there was a mix-up at the hospital?
- *Vobisne curae umquam est num in valetudinario confusio facta sit?*

At a Funeral

Remember when we only used to run into each other at weddings?
- *Meministine cum nos solum in nuptiis obviam eramus?*

FINAL LATIN

DENIQUE DIAETAM EFFICACEM INVENI
- AT LAST I HAVE FOUND A DIET THAT WORKS

NUNC, VERO INTER SAXUM ET LOCUM DURUM SUM
- NOW, I REALLY AM BETWEEN A ROCK AND A HARD PLACE

DIXI ME AEGROTARE, SED ECQUIS AUSCULTARET?
- I SAID I WAS SICK, BUT WOULD ANYBODY LISTEN?

TAM EXANIMIS QUAM TUNICA NEHRU FIO
- I AM AS DEAD AS THE NEHRU JACKET

INVICEM, RES BONA EST NON PLUS DENTHARPAGARUM
- ON THE OTHER HAND, THE GOOD NEWS IS NO MORE DENTISTRY

SIC FRIATUR CRUSTUM DULCE
- IT IS THUS THAT THE COOKIE CRUMBLES

OBESA CANTAVIT
- THE FAT LADY HAS SUNG

ABOUT
THE AUTHOR
De scriptore

HENRY BEARD spent eight harrowing years studying Latin, during which time he read selections from the works of Caesar, Cicero, Virgil, Horace, Ovid, Catullus, Plautus, Terence, and Lucretius. After co-founding the English-language periodical *National Lampoon* and writing a number of books in English, including *Sailing: A Sailor's Dictionary* and *Miss Piggy's Guide to Life*, he is happy to finally have an opportunity to make some use of his knowledge of a language that really hasn't been all that helpful over the years, except for the time he suddenly realized that the thing he was about to order from the menu of a restaurant in Rome looked an awful lot like the Latin word for "eel." Mr. Beard resides in *Novi Eboraci* (New York).